These Weighted Months

Also by Michele Fermanis-Winward
and published by Ginninderra Press

Threading Raindrops
The Eucalypt Distillery
A Larrikin in the Blood
To the Dam (Pocket Poets)
The Sail Weaver (Pocket Poets)
Curdled Milk (Pocket Poets)

Michele Fermanis-Winward

These Weighted Months

With gratitude to my editor, Brendan Doyle, for his
continued support and excellent work on my manuscript.
And to my publishers, Stephen Matthews OAM
and Brenda Eldridge of Ginninderra Press,
who believe in giving a voice to those with tales to tell.

Dedicated to my companions in Melbourne's stage four
Covid 19 restrictions, my husband and carer, Kevin,
and my assistance dog, Bella.

These Weighted Months
ISBN 978 1 76109 256 5
Copyright © text Michele Fermanis-Winward 2022

First published 2022 by
GINNINDERRA PRESS
PO Box 3461 Port Adelaide 5015
www.ginninderrapress.com.au

Contents

Foreword	9
Transmission	11
Swept Aside	13
Marking Time	14
No Immunity From Fear	15
Like a Bird	16
Crowd Control	17
Conquest	18
Who Knows Where This Will End	19
Our World Grows Small	20
The New Order	21
Bound	23
Waiting	24
Defenceless	25
Slipping Through the Cracks	26
Tumult	27
It's Black and White	28
Connected	29
Music On My Tongue	30
How to Brew a Potion	31
Weather	33
Deciduous	34
The Fifteenth	35
Crisis	36
The Faces of Love	37
Rupture	38
The Call	39
The Shell	40
No Parades Today	41

Absence	42
The Unwelcome Guest	43
Linkages	44
Until Further Notice	45
An Ordinary Saturday	46
On Beach Sand	47
Only the Signs Remain	48
When	49
In Idlib	50
Separation Anxiety	51
Dumped	52
From Convict to Covid	53
Charmed	55
Culture Shifts	56
Was it	57
Hemmed in	58
Bruegelesque	59
Day and Night	60
Masked Riders	61
State of Disaster	62
Our Friendship	63
Safe Steps	64
The Pharmacy	65
In Extremis	66
My Lady Grief	67
The Women of My Blood	68
The Burdens	69
Reproach	71
A Meditation	72
In Solitude	73
Resilient	74
The Whales Remember Their Songs	75

In Tune	76
On Living	77
For Family	78
Our Dog's Pledge	79
These Weighted Months	80
Before Today	81
On the Cusp	82
Disposable	83
Six Metres By Six	84
Scavenger	85
Homebound	86
Walking to Tomorrow	87
Home	88
Out From the Dark	89
An Unfamiliar Noise	90
This Frail Raft	91

Foreword

> We navigate to unknown reaches
> as though cast upon an ocean
> in our coracles of hide and bone
> unsure if they will hold us
> and bring us safely back to land.

Covid 19 and the year 2020, when our leaders proclaimed, 'We are all in this together.' We were told to work from home and to school our children there. A nation of travellers was grounded. The government warned us to social distance at two arm lengths apart, to isolate and then to wear a mask.

During this time, when a loved one fell ill, we could not be with them to hold their hand and offer comfort. My fiercely independent ninety-four-year-old uncle fell, not to Covid, but a stroke. We drove south to Victoria in June and found, because of border closures, we were there for five months. In Melbourne, we could not visit my uncle during the stage four restrictions and he did not understand what was happening to his life. We stayed in one small room while Covid numbers grew and fell and my uncle railed against his confinement to a nursing home. While in another part of Melbourne, my intellectually disabled brother had to learn to be self-sufficient. I, with complex mental and physical illness, attempted to act as a responsible adult, sometimes without success.

This collection is my response to a year that will stand out in all our memories.

Transmission

Through air, on sea and road
from breath, a cough or shout
the clasp of hand to touch of face
without a pause to think.

As last year neared its end
in another land a busy market thrived
the air was rank with fear and blood
cries and voices rose and merged.

Here wild creatures trussed and hung
or stacked in cages
waited to be slaughtered, sold and cooked
overflowing on the street.

One by one people disappeared
a stall holder and his customer
an old man who swept the lane
but they were quietly missed.

Then a doctor raised concern
for the patients in his care
why could no one see
this was more than winter flu.

As the new year turned
there were people crowding terminals
rushing home to celebrate
with family and friends.

The doctor stayed, was vilified
disgraced for voicing false alarms
soon the world called him a hero
and then, he too was gone.

Swept Aside

How could we know
we were still mourning
the loss and trauma'
from summer's mega fires.

For us who were not burnt
the comfort of routines
kept our lives afloat
we made plans for tomorrow.

Before the season's end
we had something else to fear
the news at night had narrowed
it focused on disease.

The virus was a wild fire
that saw doctors overwhelmed
in a regime where the army
could build hospitals in days.

Covid now is etched into our minds
we live attentive to the rules
that keep us from its path
we learn our plans were smoke and dreams.

Marking Time

A line is drawn across our days
no more idle shopping
buying things we do not need.

Gone are café breakfasts
and markets on weekends
strolling out to meet our friends
at restaurants and pubs.

We try to find our balance
on a tightrope of restrictions
which the government demands.

Street trees are turning red
without the tourist glare
everyone's at home
we wait to end our isolation.

Bitumen arteries of the world
are left to trucks transporting food
and the right engages a socialist ideal.

Money flows to keep us from despair
Centrelink queues wind round the block
our hands are out, we're asking
when can work resume.

No Immunity From Fear

The streets are silent
this eerie, before the storm expectation
waiting for our turn
we watch more powerful nations
count their dead as seniors fall.

No revolution
or mobs demanding change
we are undone
by fear of a contagion
wealth and power cannot stall.

We came together
through summer's fire and flood
now we isolate and hoard
afraid to touch our neighbours
in case they bring us plague.

Like a Bird

I crash headlong into glass
my vision of this year
has bruised and broken feathers
from an unyielding windowpane.

All I found was my reflection
enclosed in endless forest.
I leave a snatch of feathers
stuck to a splattered imprint.

Like many I was tempted
to trust what is deception
the image that I saw
was a mirror I can't enter.

Crowd Control

The Royal Easter Show
our footy and the cricket
concerts, musicals and raves
even the Olympic Games
must be postponed.

All the festivals we love
the bonds that give connection
through music, sport or church
from empty halls and stadiums
our passion is suppressed.

Life's rituals and celebrations
baby showers to funeral homes
strict limits are imposed
on who we think essential
to mark these milestones.

Conquest

We fly home to sanctuary
lock our border gates
give up our freedom
trust others with our lives.

Told we save ourselves
that disaster is the price
if we return in haste
to yesterday's society.

We expect to be reviled
or severely fined
if we step outside the rules
don't isolate ourselves.

Now we rely on government
to provide our daily needs
how easily we slip into
an authoritarian state.

Who Knows Where This Will End

On hold – our lives of mortgages
secure jobs and super funds
cheap food with basic goods
filling supermarket shelves.

Who knows where this will end

The power of mass consumption
has met a wrecking ball
we all must bear the burden
when this time has passed.

Who knows where this will end

The sick are nursed by strangers
denied a loved one's touch
it shatters our presumptions
now we are locked apart.

Who knows where this will end

Will we be stronger for the test
or will our faith be broken
by injustice, greed and stealth
that sees our woes compound.

Who knows where this will end.

Our World Grows Small

Today the news report
constricts our view
it rains health information
which floods across the globe.

Unsettled by the world
outside our neighbourhood
we are told to stay enclosed
for our life's sake.

While our favourite cafe shuts
and illness brews unseen
home no more a transit point
it is our sanctuary now.

How little we are changed
but vast the chasm
in the boundaries of trust
between today and one week past.

The New Order

When recent fires
ravaged summer months
our homes and lives
a climate in collapse
was all too evident.

Now we are locked apart
from our days' routines
the news we hear broadcast
is how we can survive
the danger to our health.

We draw comfort from
breathing unpolluted air
learn to live with less
turn back the clocks
grow our fruit and greens.

While we look inward
our coral reef expires
koalas perish without forests
and coal mines expand
to foul our aquifers.

Laws pass unopposed
they leave us vulnerable
to fascist intent
a police state empties streets
no protest is allowed.

When we are free
to raise our voice again
will we find a better place
or will our planet
be deeper in the mire.

Bound

We are the wind-up painted bird
soldered to its perch
the air within balloons
threatened by a pin
tadpoles in their shrinking pond.

We watch events unfold
not knowing when or if
this new ordeal will end
can life be as it was
or shall we all be changed.

Waiting

Another world war
sweeps across the globe
there are no guns or bombs
but we are told, seek shelter
for you are now in peril.

This invader comes
by plane and boat
spreads on the air we breathe
or a loved one's held embrace
there is no defence.

We watch as other nations
lock their border gates
with economies in tatters
we listen to the tally
and know our turn will come.

Defenceless

No super jets nor submarines
no border force
with refugees in offshore jails
our high-cost weapons
cannot protect us now
this danger comes under radar screens.

Each nation has its own routines
of cafes, bistros and iconic pubs
from music halls to sporting grounds
all clubs must close their doors
in local gyms hi-tech machines no longer beep
no promenades along the strand tonight.

We sit at home, explore
the darkest reaches of our freezer chests
experiment with sago balls
find out how much a pack of lentils gives
try not to think of what tomorrow holds
we know there's worse before it ends.

Slipping Through the Cracks

Gaps appear in news broadcasts
I grieve for those we cannot hear
the ones who fall from light
far from our TV screens.

Top dogs spruik their mega plans
and we are blitzed against our will
by schemes for mines and gas
while someone small tips out of sight.

A student trapped without support
the homeless girl afraid at night
of being knifed by her ex
refugees wasting years in jail.

In our western sandy desert
a cave with fifty thousand years
recording living history
is blown to rubble in the dark.

Tumult

I feel the clench
a tightening in my lungs
it pulses to my belly's pit
an ache that stops all thought
and strips my heart of joy.

The image of a trust betrayed
injustice by the state
or cruelty to any living thing
sends shockwaves through my core
and rises to a scream inside my throat.

It's Black and White

In the USA
deaths from Covid grow
and people queue for food
the poor have less immunity
more black families mourn than white.

On TV – hands in pockets
casually a white cop kneels
upon a black man's neck
he calmly waits, does not look down
until the man goes limp.

And here where mining giants rule
they overpower the people's rights
ignore our ancient tribal art
bomb cultural sites and native title land
build gates to keep the locals out.

A people whom we should revere
the oldest living culture that exists today
subsist on government cheques
in squalor and neglect and in our jails
more black families mourn than white.

Connected

Enclosed inside familiar rooms
both small and large
we move in greater circles
among our facebook friends.

You invite me in
we share our best
both intimate and broad
it soothes the rupture to our days.

We are a string of jewels
held by the wifi thread
each one of us sustained
by the constancy of love.

Music On My Tongue

l want to cook again
some find it a daily chore
coming after hours of work
for me it is a game of chance.

More than mere sustenance
I must extemporise
with jumbled notes as flavours clash
my taste buds sense cacophony.

Now from the dark
forsaken corners of my shelves
come turmeric and cardamom
mustard seeds rolling on the bench.

The mysteries of tamarind paste
and saffron strands unfold
they perform a sensuous slow dance
create this melody I cannot repeat.

How to Brew a Potion

I gather bright calendulas
as their flowers open
I wait for bees to forage
these gems of earth and sun.

Then I harvest rosemary spikes
and strip the leaves from stems
their sticky oil on fingers
holds a penetrating scent.

I search a large bay tree
its fruit is plump green balls
ripe berries shrink
turn into blackened drupes.

These herbs I smother
in virgin olive oil
set on a windowsill
and tend them for a week.

Now on the lowest flame
I watch as tiny bubbles burst
and orange petals fade
slide into ochre brown.

Slowly stirred for an hour
I strain the oil with care
add beeswax tears
pot up and wait one more day.

This is what our ancients used
a Greek and Roman panacea
the lore of healing plants
of worshipping the natural world.

How many women had to burn
because they had a gift to share
my salve is ready now to serve
and I am proud to call myself
a novice of the witch's art.

Weather

We shelter in our homes
knowing they are safe
from wild danger's grasp
as winds rise in the east.

The bureau forecasts snow
branches no longer tremble
they lash a soft grey sky
snapping weaker stems.

As treetops crash together
against the weight of clouds
eucalypts' blue shadows
cast twilight into rooms.

Red maple leaves break free
they dart among the bushes
like startled wrens
wanting shelter from the storm.

Deciduous

We drop like autumn leaves
the young and old
yesterday we thought the days
were made for us to spend.

Suddenly the sky grows dark
cold winds blow us about
we feel a weakness in our veins
hear crackling as we move.

We are thick upon the ground
and watch our numbers grow
hope we are the lucky ones
reborn as evergreens on earth.

The Fifteenth

Beware the Ides of March
in ancient Rome it was year's end
a scapegoat would be found and purged
it was the deadline to repay a debt
and the day that Julius Caesar died.

The day I said, I'll see you soon
to friends, the café and the gym
and all the shops in our small town
we thought two weeks at best
was all that we would need apart.

Now it's been sixty days
of isolation in our homes
adept with masks and gloves
a disinfectant in my bag
I'm good at social distance.

No trips to see my family
no scenic drives out west
prepared to answer to police
if I am stopped on the road
without permitted reason.

I've checked the bank
with no account outstanding
no knife held at my back
this purge is now worldwide
it makes scapegoats of us all.

Crisis

Like the war our parents knew
basic foods are rationed
luxury goods no longer rate
they gather dust in bolted shops.

We step from all our yesterdays
to danger at our door
no carefree days outside
until the threat is quashed.

Shades of a bygone age
when townsfolk stayed at home
a curfew set upon their steps
enforced by crown and church.

Restrictions mount
we live as in a sci-fi movie set
where lives disintegrate
while the valiant carry on.

Like pigs inside a house of straw
the wolf we call the virus
is howling to be fed
and we must sit and quake.

The Faces of Love

A word, a meaning, a world
spreading out from our hearts
a balm against the mob
the ones who hate.

Do good we're told – spread light
upon this troubled globe
we are overwhelmed
by all who need our care.

To keep our hearts intact
we build a wall against
the battering ram of another's love
that looks to us like hate.

Rupture

Fault lines appear
across the landscape of our lives
we are caught
and cannot bridge the gap
to all we held before.

We learn to hibernate
like northern bears
slow motion through our days
ask to wake in spring
a bud opening with life.

Things we left behind
our friends, our favourite haunts
the pastimes we enjoyed
when we return
their value will be changed.

The Call

It may come at any hour
a stranger's voice down the line
someone you love is gravely ill
you hear the list
of broken bones and worse.

The measured rhythm of your days
becomes cacophony and disarray
in panic to be at their side
your hand in theirs to reassure
this battle is not fought alone.

The Shell

You smile but do not see
as I approach your bed
bruises linger from a sudden fall
that changed the world for you.

The voice I know so well
still sounds the same
worn thin with use
but you're not there.

You're swimming in the past
out of your depth with life
and you can only glimpse
odd moments of today.

I'm looking for a reel
to bring you back to shore
where you can know who I am
and start the road to home.

This place you find yourself
makes no sense to you
elusive as the waves
that roll inside your head.

No Parades Today

We have been sent away
by cycle, train and tram
city life flutters then grows quiet.
Once Melbourne's vibrant heart
would draw the millions in.

How long before its festivals
parades with cheering crowds
will throng for us again
now iconic laneways
fill shadows with our ghosts.

The scent of brewing coffee
of pasta, spice and crêpes
no longer curls from café doors
no lunchtime press
with diners spilling onto streets.

City fathers cast in bronze
look down from granite pedestals
with lonely vacant stares
at the few who hurry past
no loitering allowed.

The grand department stores
have moved to trade online
office workers nine to five at home
and gold rush palaces
wait to breathe again.

Absence

Tonight at ten
we stroll deserted streets
she's in and out of open gates
exploring all the smells
that any dog would love.

I gaze up to lighted squares
where people in apartment rooms
watch TV screens and fold their clothes
unaware the street below
is empty but for me and she.

Never has it been like this
our ordinary urban space
made for and by humanity
now man has been removed
it echoes with abandoned life.

The Unwelcome Guest

I would come to town and wonder
perchance it was my brother
or a cousin or a friend
who was clumsy with my things
when I found them chipped and cracked.

We have been in isolation here
for over three months now
each week I find something else
damaged by an unseen hand
it's the poltergeist I say.

Perhaps it lurks within the stove
or underneath the sink
but never where I seek
we are no longer isolated
there is a butter-fingered stranger
hiding in our flat.

Linkages

No lumpy rise of distant land
a perfect seam joins sky to bay
the city grid holds tram lines taut
their wires above our heads
a buzzing cage for birds to dodge.

North and South main roads
from town to far inland
fling wide their arms and legs
connecting villages to coast
along the flat sand tracks.

Lycra clad the cyclists speed
in and out between parked cars
no backward safety glance
as drivers brake and curse
along the bends and straights.

The mass of high-rise homes
sharp edged in glass and steel
obscures old bluestone lanes
now wastes that catch
our limp discarded masks.

Until Further Notice

Shops are closed
once I would browse
the local artists' store
and our design emporium.

There I would admire
a soft green celadon
the satin feel of glaze
and curve of lip
that makes a well turned jug.

Then on impulse
I must claim it as my own
knowing I had others
on my shelves to use.

Now I feel deprived
with only factory produced
supermarket fare
to satisfy my hungry senses.

Spotlit pictures on a screen
must do the work of touch
the translucent wonder
of handmade porcelain
cannot be expressed.

I do not cradle in my hands
the measure of a craft
years of quiet devotion
to create the perfect jug.

An Ordinary Saturday

Masked and walking hand in hand
along our sandy beaches
masks on cyclists and skaters
as we practice social distance
there are children in the shallows
parents watching from the shore.

It could be any weekend afternoon
except for the restrictions
aware our lives and those we love
depend on strict compliance
this is how war controls a people
it makes dictators out of doctors.

On Beach Sand

Still it washes up
charred twigs from summer's burning
that now seems long ago.

A swallow swoops and reels
above the storm-racked beach
while we below are stranded.

So much has washed from drains
from all that we abandon
with our lives enclosed and wanting.

Those who thought to fly
find their wings are clipped
our spring has yet to come.

All our bright tomorrows
held back in masks and gloves
this winter stays too long.

Only the Signs Remain

Driving down Beach Road
from St Kilda to Seaford
through towns that line the bay
their old-style shopping strips.
Once a crush of cars moved past
the smart and shabby stores.

Few cars hinder us today
shops are bolted ghosts
their stock is left on hold
the takeaway, bank and chemist
are trading for the few
compelled to venture out.

The state and nation wait
to see if cases drop
trust our leaders know the path
back to lives we left behind
before these unreal times
and our economy collapsed.

When

this time has passed
and all our vulnerable
have been protected
when a vaccine is provided
to everyone on earth.

How changed our world will be
the hugs and kisses freely given
withheld by habits formed in isolation
we laugh behind our palms
handshakes no longer seen.

We shop by standing back
to let another pass
and do not lean on counters
refrain from handling stock
wash everything we buy.

We disinfect ourselves
and everything we touch
sanitisers found by doors
in cars and always in our bags
how clean we have become.

No germs or lurking virus
will snatch our lives again.

In Idlib

Here streets are twisted metal
and mounds of broken concrete
there is a woman
like any other you might see
bent by years of toil.

She cares for sixteen orphans
left by her rebel sons
she is boiling beans and lentils
the older children are out working
here food is luxury.

Covid only matters in the markets
making prices rise
a boy of ten would like to read and write
but school's a luxury as well
he works for medicine and milk.

While in the basement
beneath their shattered home
his grandmother cooks
and cleans and cares
a luxury for other Idlib orphans.

Separation Anxiety

Do you remember
what we said in March
two weeks of isolation
is all that it should take
to save us from disease.

Last December
in bush-ringed villages and towns
we bonded as communities
to fight the mega fires
that threatened all our homes.

We remain in isolation
inside those very homes
avoiding groups and friends
the fear of contagion
divides our neighbourhoods.

Now it is mid August
and we have learnt to make
an island of our home
soon it will be summer
who will help us if it burns.

Dumped

We are motley, masked and curious
scavengers and walkers
standing on the corner
picking over goods that made a home.

There's a baby bouncer and a pram
tables, chairs and pressure cooker
each Wednesday afternoon
another heap appears.

Much like the weeks before
a garbage truck tomorrow
will clear it all away
their owner has moved on.

To somewhere rent is cheaper
or to Mum or just couch surfing
who can tell in Covid times
I turn away and call my dog.

I am haunted by the question
was this an eviction
or a better place was offered
to the mother and her child.

From Convict to Covid

The men came in their thousands
wrenched from English slums
sent to live in wilderness
they had to forge new families
from the strangers close at hand.

The lure of gold
brought madness to men's eyes
the diggings were a siren's song
teams of men tore at the earth
forged bonds against the law.

Outback the drovers ranged
long paddocks and their lonely weeks
to drive the herds along
with billies boiled and tales exchanged
under a bunyip moon.

Cobber, digger, mate, in pain and need
through Flanders trenches soldiers wept
for remnants of their lost humanity
'for pity's sake, don't leave me here to die'
they cried to friends who got them out.

In jungle sweat and ragged clothes
empty bellies and weeping sores
prison gangs shared all they had
joked and japed to salve brutality
'you bloody stay alive to spite those Nips'.

At RSLs they honoured fallen chums
marched on Anzac Day
humped a bluey through the bush
moved around the shearers' camps,
crowded in to cheer their footy codes.

As men mocked wowsers and tall poppy chumps
they helped to build each other's homes
knew that burdens would be shared
how easy then to say to us
another's fate is in our hands.

When we are told
'Stay home to save your parents' lives
don't spread contagion round'
our gift for being mates not virulent,
has always seen us through.

Charmed

I used to see her up the road
sitting outside shops
they shared a rug for warmth
me with my Bella
wary when we passed
as she pulled her dog in close.

The state has found compassion
giving homes to people on the street
girls don't want the kind of freedom
that sleeping rough can bring
now she is my neighbour
flat four to me at number three.

Her dog's a big brown hound
my Bella's small and aged
a dozen women and their dogs
are living in our block
some dogs are not as friendly
seeing Bella as their prey.

Chocky's always charming
and will visit us sometimes
checks out my Bella's bowl
though she doesn't touch a thing
but there's always something tasty
in my pocket for a friend.

Culture Shifts

A winning smile
no longer rates
we now judge warmth
by wrinkles next to eyes
above the rule of cloth.

At the beach
dogs rush to greet each other
we stand discreetly back
express relief to have their love
to get us through these troubles.

The rats and crows
grow bolder on the streets
but rubbish now is missing.
Once bins had overflowed
along this tourist strip.

Life has become
a solitary pursuit
for those who exercise.
Jaunts to the shops with coffee after
are burdens only one may carry.

Was it

the Depression and the war
when they were young
that set their thwarted lives
and kept them bound for years.

She would be an artist
he a professional sportsman
but those were invitations
that never came again.

Their dreams were riches
they would never reap
the chances given others
left them far behind.

How many like my parents
with careers on hold today
as they wait in isolation
will find their chances fade.

Hemmed in

These too familiar walls
no gallery halls to bring relief
nor restaurant meals by candlelight
our shopping is curtailed to food
and online facebook leads.

There is a sense of gratitude
numbers here are small
but lives we worked so hard to build
are foxed and set aside
old routines fade into sepia.

Extroverts sport stylish masks
as none can see their face
without a risk to health
we all endure our dose of fear
news comes in lists and tolls.

Inhale and out through filtered cloth
my lungs feel trapped
I dare not cough or sneeze
until the hours are mine again
and l can lounge outside this tiny flat.

Bruegelesque

The sky is grey and chill
softly howling past my door
a wind drawn from Antarctica
finds us wrapped against the cold
recalls a scene of lowland ice and snow.

As we strive to stay intact
days blur in locked-down rooms
I am transported back through time
to a painted medieval scene
of parables and plague.

Here the ways of ordinary life
continue on the edge
while we go stumbling blindly on
with hope someone can see ahead
to lead us clear of harm.

The sky turns darker still
rain squalls are churning
the last of fallen leaves.
I look for peasants bundling twigs
down Melbourne's bluestone lanes.

Day and Night

The three of us
locked down in one small flat
I step outside after dark
the streets are bare in winter quiet
a tracery of leafless trees
hard shadows on the ground
lights glare from corner posts.

We live with shields upon our breath
move aside and do not speak
to pass another on a walk
hope that none will come too close
with no excuse to feel at ease
until the danger's passed
I return to our secluded space.

Masked Riders

The days are slicked by rain
that drizzles through to night
then bikes are heard
the constant hiss of wheels
passing up and down.

Led by a flickering lamp
young men in masks
heads bent and pedalling fast
the streets are dinner lines
no cars to dodge tonight.

From balconies of storeyed flats
meals ordered in lockdown
there's curry, pizza, chips
stowed in a padded box
speeding to our doors.

One rain-soaked cyclist halts
our bell is rung and all we see
are eyes above a mask
he can feel the warmth
coming from our rooms.

He taps a mobile screen
then turns his wheels around
the night has just begun
and as we dine
he's counting tips and hours.

State of Disaster

Now we face a curfew
from eight to five a.m.
the image conjures war
and totalitarian rule.

The anonymity of masks
to shield our individuality
new rules have been imposed
to protect us from ourselves.

No travel over five kilometres
and only one per household shops
one hour for exercise per day
we pause, exhale and compromise.

Our Friendship

Your eyes were filled with light
each time we met
enclosing me in your arms
the warmth of empathy
and sorrows shared.

You placed your hand on mine
as we talked, sitting close
with secrets whispered
for our ears alone
side by side exchanging warmth.

The years have bound us tight
through love and trust
no jealousy or fights
but now because of Covid
we can no longer meet.

Safe Steps

We learn to duck and weave
within our captive breath
under the mask we smile
step aside to let an elder pass
their muffled thanks or nod
or sad averted gaze.

By the door we keep
sanitiser and a pack of gloves
to walk around the block
and exercise our dogs
they're allowed to touch a friend
but we alas are not.

The Pharmacy

By the door there is a guard
in uniform, thermometer at hand
a card pass on a cord around his neck
he checks my card and temperature
permits me and my dog to pass.

Sent to the back, we desperados wait
some pace the floor or rock, I twitch
Bella tugging at her lead
the paperwork for my meds
has come from my home state.

The girl beside me nods
whispers 'what shall I steal today'
and deftly pockets eucalyptus oil
I sense without the need to look
the chemist has her clocked.

A momentary break
while tapping at her screen
a message sent down the front
to intercept the miscreant
and say she can't come back.

There's tears, she wails,
'don't cross me off your list'
they make her wait
I hold my breath, look distressed
and hope they will relent.

In Extremis

We came together
to fight the summer fires
communities renewed their bonds
shared all they could
cried in each other's arms.

After the ash and ember storms
had settled to the ground
our masks were set aside
then on the air
a new contagion blew.

By law we stand apart
and close our doors
claim sanctuary inside our homes
fear brewed by mounting tolls
we mask ourselves again.

How long the hours become
with lack of work or play
our lives made small
in the shadows of monotony
minds turning to despair.

The days we once enjoyed
are relics of the past
we're told a cure will come
but will it be too late
for the heavy months endured.

My Lady Grief

She is my life's companion
in the darkened room at night
before release to sleep.

She is the ache inside my head
a heaviness in my arms
and depth within my eyes.

She prefers interiors
the tightness in my lungs
a knot inside my belly.

She fills the quiet moments
at any time of day or night
silence is her dominion.

She requires solitude
and demands no competition
I have become her servant.

Contemplation feeds her
she becomes a flooding river
until I'm sure to drown.

I can escape her though
outside among the living green
in a garden under sun or cloud.

I pray she does not multiply
or send her sisters out
and overwhelm the earth.

The Women of My Blood

We survive
not through gains but loss
it filters through our veins
from a forebear sent to Tarban Creek
to me at John of God.

The voices in our heads
preach we deserve to die
we cringe inside our shells
like snails upon a step
we live by acts of chance.

Police and those in charge
do not see our fear
we will be crushed without a thought
are always on our guard
for the shadow on our path.

There are many such as us
who live with mind's distress
the seclusions of today
set us against ourselves
with nowhere safe to hide.

The Burdens

This year we witnessed firestorms
with towns consumed by flames
the loss continues on and on
now in the grip of Covid
we know our lives have changed.

The body remembers
trauma etched onto its cells
we pass these to our children
a malleable legacy
they craft as misery or strength.

When I see a highland piper in the mist
or hear a colleen at her harp
or stand on Tassie's cold west coast
then my blood will not be quiet
my heart must fall apart.

I bore the highland clearances
my body ached with cold
no home or hearth to keep me warm
the baby died in my womb
and we were sold abroad.

I was an Irish mother
inside my clothes I shrank to bone
prayed as my children starved
famine broke the family bonds
with none to ease our plight.

Sent to Van Diemen's Land
I felt the lash against my back
but hunger is a powerful cure
for wilfulness and pride
my past fades in to distant memory.

Each day I strive to change
the traumas in my heritage
create a work of gratitude
from the struggles they survived
sometimes all I do is weep.

Reproach

I am given this pause
to reflect or weep
for what I might have done.

It is the rising wind
that churns with malice
tearing at a fragile self-esteem.

It is the voice that will not quiet
nagging in the dark
saying 'you are not enough'.

It is a landscape in ruin
of all I could not mend
or remedy with love.

A Meditation

Surrender
let your body sink
towards the ground
feel its warmth beneath your head.

Cushioned by the soft red sand
that once looked down
as mountain crags
now it holds the dust of countless lives.

The scent of ants
are those you crushed
as they went on their way
unaware you towered overhead.

The wind you hear
scrolling through the trees
is a song of praise
gives thanks for every living thing.

The large and small
in all their sounds and forms
will come together in the end
as dust or ash or grains of soft red sand.

In Solitude

I am soothed by isolation
the distractions of noise
that feed our world
are muted in my sanctuary.

Still the heart grieves
how could it not
when so much loss exists
and forecasts more tomorrow.

In the turning of a patch of soil
my planting out of herbs and weeds
I am given a meditation
on taking and receiving life.

Resilient

I stride the bitumen
newly laid and glossy black.

Perhaps a week has passed
now grape and mint, sweet violets
are breaking through the crust.

It could not smother them
Melbournites survive.

The Whales Remember Their Songs

They are listening to the change
deep within the rumbling dark
a novel silence grows.

Past islands' shimmering palms
spread through the ocean waves
new sounds begins to rise.

Whales can hear once more
they call across the leagues
reaching all their children far away.

Connecting round the globe
from ice to tropic lands
the whales are chorusing again.

Sharing what they almost lost
when hum and throb of mega ships
drowned out their ancient songs.

In Tune

I hear a low persistent beat
soft pounding in my ears
outside the streets are bare.

A dog lets out a solitary bark
a bird whistles overhead
then silence once again.

Both comforting and rare
the beats continue side by side
my heart and Mother Earth.

On Living

I did not expect to grow old
death pursued me as a child
but here I am, an elderly woman
trailing my share of sorrow
triumph and delight.

Having seen its face
I do not fear death
only asking for this year
to complete the tasks
that filter through my head.

I will never be cold
each day I face
is wrapped with love
made from strands of caring
by family and friends.

For Family

We sacrifice each day
and put our lives on hold
connect by voice and text
to those we cannot touch.

Warmth comes down the line
the caring we all seek
with love expressed in words
we ask, are you all right.

But what we yearn for most
is to know that you are safe
that when we speak again
an embrace is all you need.

Our Dog's Pledge

I am a sanctuary for the soul
the sun when you are deep in cloud
warmth when you feel chilled.

I teach you life is brief
though my blaze of light
will never leave your heart.

As we sit together through the night
I will provide the balm
to calm your deepest fears.

These Weighted Months

We are hoping
and always we are waiting
like a myriad others
in so many other places.

We wrote wishes for tomorrow
on the parchment of our hearts
but this misadventure
is causing them to fade.

We can no longer read
with the eyes of yesterday
and we are asked
to wait and wait again.

We feel heavy in our limbs
as the seasons change
our wishes for tomorrow
are scratchings in the dark.

Before Today

The young tomorrow
will not understand the way it was
but you remember.

How we once greeted strangers
by shaking hands
we would kiss and hug a friend.

Breathing in each other's faces
the crush when listening to bands
student parties and jostling of crowds.

The heat of protest marches
standing arm in arm and chanting
the festivals and peak hour trams.

We would be on guard
for the nudge of a pickpocket
and men with groping hands.

And everyone would catch
a cold and flu in winter
how careless we were then.

On the Cusp

Pear and plum trees in full bloom
our busy shopping malls
are dormant, cold and empty
their winter sales abandoned.

Trees are swathed in vibrant green
as I cross the empty road
no need to wait for cars to pass
the tram arrives and I ride alone.

A few masked shoppers hurry past
no browsing only dodging rain
I step inside the market hall
today birdsong is heard outside.

Fresh food is keeping stalls alive
the rest are darkened alleyways
barricades block the path ahead
and a scent of jasmine fills my lungs.

Under eaves in quiet corners
once filled with glare and noise
small birds now build their nests
reclaiming what we leave,

while we are chrysalis or nymph
held in suspended animation
unsure if we will waken
as butterflies or locusts.

Disposable

I see them snagged on bushes
within our pocket parks
crumpled in the gutters
and clinging to the edge of drains.

They festoon our narrow lanes
like discarded chocolate wrappers
or fast food boxes
before we all stayed home.

The symbols of this year
like the signs on bolted doors
and the many lives on hold
are abandoned paper masks.

Six Metres By Six

From winter blasts to spring
three months in one small room
four walls to hold our lives.

One hour per day
to stretch our limbs
outside of this confinement.

The three of us like shadows
that spiral in an updraft
try not to be entangled.

We accommodate
the barbs of irritation
in a space too small for conflict.

Scavenger

I look for treasure
amid small plots of ground
part building rubble
and discarded rubbish
there's twisted wire and bottle tops
rusting in the dirt

detritus of construction sites
carried by the rain and leaking drains
down bluestone gutters
among the sharps
and broken plastic shapes
there is much to glean

I am getting a street cred
the woman with red hair
and her aged dog
we patter slowly round
a nod, g'day and I feel safe
down dead end alleyways.

On the beach
arabesques of driftwood scraps
caught in stranded weed
water pounded coloured glass
and bits of pot and stone
for collages I weave.

Homebound

In March
the first few cases
came onto our shores
from returning travellers
hosting this new disease.

In June
a medical emergency
took us interstate
it is September now
with borders tightly closed.

We do not see ourselves
getting home this year
we stay but cannot visit
the uncle left in crisis
whom we came to aid.

Strangers must provide for him
my uncle does not understand
the nursing care he needs
knowledge of the virus
quickly passed him by.

He thinks I'm cruel not visiting
or letting him go home
and believes he has not changed.
If we can quarantine our land
can I quarantine my heart.

Walking to Tomorrow

These days lack definition
changing with the clouds
dependent on contagion's spread
and if its numbers climb.

I try to distance from my heart
to live within the landscape of my craft
the chasms of uncertainty
I rarely venture down.

Routines are what I crave
their paths are gentle slopes
terrain I've walked for many years
and my feet are safe upon.

Will I know myself
beyond the patterns that I hold today
or when this time has ceased
will I lose my step
and fall to new unknowns.

Home

This faraway other place
that we have been denied,
our years of sanctuary
within its much loved walls.

It holds the story of our lives
our triumphs and our grief
it protects the secrets
that no one else can hear.

We try to compensate
pretend we do not mind
glad to wear a mask
so none can see our pain.

Out From the Dark

Each day there spreads
a bloom of palest green
it's colouring our days
down narrow lanes
on tram-coursed boulevards
and cold suburban roads.

Towards the warming light
an irresistible urge to grow
is bursting into bud
unfurling tight-bound leaves
while we are watching
kept closed and locked inside.

An Unfamiliar Noise

I hear shouting in the street
laughter spilling from cafés
patrons' eyes squeeze in delight.

A festival is underway
as we celebrate release
from the silence of our thoughts.

Free to meet outside with friends
to indulge at restaurants
to see loved ones again.

Shops are turning on their lights
music calling us inside
to spend and spend some more.

These lucky ones with jobs
while others stay at home
mourn all we could not save.

This Frail Raft

we set our lives upon
not knowing where the journey ends
our choice, to fall in love with chance
or wait for clear signposts.

We hope the choices made
are first or second best
believe that we can mend
the damage we have wrought.

We trust the stars, the sun and wind
will still be in the sky
to lead us to the shore
for we cannot turn back.

www.ingramcontent.com/pod-product-compliance
Lightning Source LLC
Chambersburg PA
CBHW062141100526
44589CB00014B/1647